Friendly Chemistry Manip

Designed by Dr. Joey Hajda anc

Copyright 2011

MW01283963

PLEASE READ THESE INSTRUCTIONS <u>FIRST</u> BEFORE CUTTING OUT ANY CARDS!

This booklet contains 4 card sets which accompany the *Friendly Chemistry* curriculum. In addition to the card sets, the cover of this booklet serves as the Doo-Wop Board™ which is the learning tool that teaches how electrons are arranged in atoms. Using scissors, cut out each page of this booklet and then carefully cut apart all of the cards. We strongly suggest you laminate these cards to improve their durability. Collecting them into sets using zip-lock bags is recommended. Note at the bottom of each page is a footer which tells which type of card is found on that page.

On the reverse side of this page you will find a die to be assembled in order to play Compound Intensity, a board game found in the course. After cutting out the die, fold it into a cube shape. Then use scotch tape to secure the cube. Cover the cube completely with tape to make a durable die. Store the die in the same bag as the Compound Intensity cards.

Once all of the card pages are removed, the cover can be laid out flat. Note on the cover there are 48 small circles (24 red and 24 white) along the lower edge. Cut along the horizontal line above these circles and then carefully cut-out the small circles. The small circles represent electrons and are referred to as "doo-wops" in the *Friendly Chemistry* text. Using a ziplock bag to collect these "doo-wops" is a recommended idea. These "doo-wops" may also be used as markers when playing the various bingo games found in the course. <u>DO NOT cut out any of the circles found above the horizontal line. These circles are used on the board to represent locations where electrons can be found.</u>

Please note that, like the other components of the *Friendly Chemistry* curriculum, the cover and contents of this booklet are copyright protected. <u>No portion of this booklet, includ-ing the cover, may be duplicated in any way without the permission of the authors.</u> Questions regarding this set of manipulatives may be directed to hideaway1@gpcom.net or call 308-870-4686.

Die for playing Compound Intensity Board Game.

1. Cut along outer edge.

2. Fold into cube shape. See diagram.

3. Use clear Scotch tape to create a cube. Cover entire cube with clear tape.

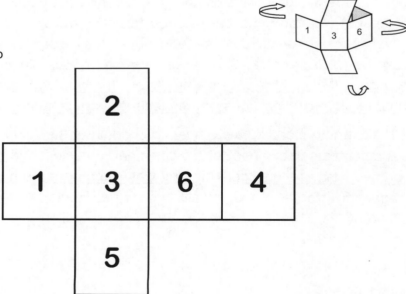

	2		
1	3	6	4
	5		

Cyanide	Permanga-nate	Copper (I)	Mercury (I)
Cyanide	Permanga-nate	Copper (I)	Mercury (I)
Cyanide	Permanga-nate	Copper (I)	Mercury (I)
Cyanide	Permanga-nate	Copper (I)	Mercury (I)

Hg^{+1}	Cu^{+1}	$(MnO_4)^{-1}$	$(CN)^{-1}$
Hg^{+1}	Cu^{+1}	$(MnO_4)^{-1}$	$(CN)^{-1}$
Hg^{+1}	Cu^{+1}	$(MnO_4)^{-1}$	$(CN)^{-1}$
Hg^{+1}	Cu^{+1}	$(MnO_4)^{-1}$	$(CN)^{-1}$

Ion Flashcards

Hydroxide	Nitrate	Nitrite	Acetate
Hydroxide	Nitrate	Nitrite	Acetate
Hydroxide	Nitrate	Nitrite	Acetate
Hydroxide	Nitrate	Nitrite	Acetate

$(C_2H_3O_2)^{-1}$	$(NO_2)^{-1}$	$(NO_3)^{-1}$	$(OH)^{-1}$
$(C_2H_3O_2)^{-1}$	$(NO_2)^{-1}$	$(NO_3)^{-1}$	$(OH)^{-1}$
$(C_2H_3O_2)^{-1}$	$(NO_2)^{-1}$	$(NO_3)^{-1}$	$(OH)^{-1}$
$(C_2H_3O_2)^{-1}$	$(NO_2)^{-1}$	$(NO_3)^{-1}$	$(OH)^{-1}$

Ion Flashcards

Sodium Ion	Potassium Ion	Lithium Ion	Cesium Ion
Sodium Ion	Potassium Ion	Lithium Ion	Cesium Ion
Sodium Ion	Potassium Ion	Lithium Ion	Cesium Ion
Sodium Ion	Potassium Ion	Lithium Ion	Cesium Ion

Cs^{+1}	Li^{+1}	K^{+1}	Na^{+1}
Cs^{+1}	Li^{+1}	K^{+1}	Na^{+1}
Cs^{+1}	Li^{+1}	K^{+1}	Na^{+1}
Cs^{+1}	Li^{+1}	K^{+1}	Na^{+1}

Ion Flashcards

Hypochlorite	Chlorite	Chlorate	Perchlorate
Hypochlorite	Chlorite	Chlorate	Perchlorate
Hypochlorite	Chlorite	Chlorate	Perchlorate
Hypochlorite	Chlorite	Chlorate	Perchlorate

$(ClO_4)^{-1}$	$(ClO_3)^{-1}$	$(ClO_2)^{-1}$	$(ClO_1)^{-1}$
$(ClO_4)^{-1}$	$(ClO_3)^{-1}$	$(ClO_2)^{-1}$	$(ClO_1)^{-1}$
$(ClO_4)^{-1}$	$(ClO_3)^{-1}$	$(ClO_2)^{-1}$	$(ClO_1)^{-1}$
$(ClO_4)^{-1}$	$(ClO_3)^{-1}$	$(ClO_2)^{-1}$	$(ClO_1)^{-1}$

Ion Flashcards

Fluoride	Chloride	Bromide	Iodide
Fluoride	Chloride	Bromide	Iodide
Fluoride	Chloride	Bromide	Iodide
Fluoride	Chloride	Bromide	Iodide

I^{-1}	Br^{-1}	Cl^{-1}	F^{-1}
I^{-1}	Br^{-1}	Cl^{-1}	F^{-1}
I^{-1}	Br^{-1}	Cl^{-1}	F^{-1}
I^{-1}	Br^{-1}	Cl^{-1}	F^{-1}

Ion Flashcards

Hydrogen Ion	Silver Ion	Ammonium Ion	Hydronium Ion
Hydrogen Ion	Silver Ion	Ammonium Ion	Hydronium Ion
Hydrogen Ion	Silver Ion	Ammonium Ion	Hydronium Ion
Hydrogen Ion	Silver Ion	Ammonium Ion	Hydronium Ion

$(H_3O)^{+1}$	$(NH_4)^{+1}$	Ag^{+1}	H^{+1}
$(H_3O)^{+1}$	$(NH_4)^{+1}$	Ag^{+1}	H^{+1}
$(H_3O)^{+1}$	$(NH_4)^{+1}$	Ag^{+1}	H^{+1}
$(H_3O)^{+1}$	$(NH_4)^{+1}$	Ag^{+1}	H^{+1}

Ion Flashcards

Sulfide	Sulfide	Sulfite	Sulfite
Sulfide	Sulfide	Sulfite	Sulfite

$(SO_3)^{-2}$	$(SO_3)^{-2}$	S^{-2}	S^{-2}
$(SO_3)^{-2}$	$(SO_3)^{-2}$	S^{-2}	S^{-2}

Sulfate	Sulfate	Carbonate	Carbonate
Sulfate	Sulfate	Carbonate	Carbonate

$(CO_3)^{-2}$	$(CO_3)^{-2}$	$(SO_4)^{-2}$	$(SO_4)^{-2}$
$(CO_3)^{-2}$	$(CO_3)^{-2}$	$(SO_4)^{-2}$	$(SO_4)^{-2}$

Ion Flashcards

Peroxide	Peroxide	Chromate	Chromate
Peroxide	Peroxide	Chromate	Chromate

$(CrO_4)^{-2}$	$(CrO_4)^{-2}$	$(O_2)^{-2}$	$(O_2)^{-2}$
$(CrO_4)^{-2}$	$(CrO_4)^{-2}$	$(O_2)^{-2}$	$(O_2)^{-2}$

Ion Flashcards

Strontium Ion	Strontium Ion	Magnesium Ion	Magnesium Ion
Strontium Ion	Strontium Ion	Magnesium Ion	Magnesium Ion

Mg^{+2}	Mg^{+2}	Sr^{+2}	Sr^{+2}
Mg^{+2}	Mg^{+2}	Sr^{+2}	Sr^{+2}

Ion Flashcards

Barium Ion	Barium Ion	Cobalt (II) Ion	Cobalt (II) Ion
Barium Ion	Barium Ion	Cobalt (II) Ion	Cobalt (II) Ion

Co^{+2}	Co^{+2}	Ba^{+2}	Ba^{+2}
Co^{+2}	Co^{+2}	Ba^{+2}	Ba^{+2}

Ion Flashcards

Nickel Ion	Nickel Ion	Zinc Ion	Zinc Ion
Nickel Ion	Nickel Ion	Zinc Ion	Zinc Ion

Zn^{+2}	Zn^{+2}	Ni^{+2}	Ni^{+2}
Zn^{+2}	Zn^{+2}	Ni^{+2}	Ni^{+2}

Ion Flashcards

Dichromate Ion	Dichromate Ion	Lead (II)	Lead (II)
Dichromate Ion	Dichromate Ion	Lead (II)	Lead (II)

Pb^{+2}	Pb^{+2}	$(Cr_2O_7)^{-2}$	$(Cr_2O_7)^{-2}$
Pb^{+2}	Pb^{+2}	$(Cr_2O_7)^{-2}$	$(Cr_2O_7)^{-2}$

| Copper (II) | Copper (II) | Iron (II) | Iron (II) |
| Copper (II) | Copper (II) | Iron (II) | Iron (II) |

Fe^{+2}	Fe^{+2}	Cu^{+2}	Cu^{+2}
Fe^{+2}	Fe^{+2}	Cu^{+2}	Cu^{+2}

Ion Flashcards

Calcium Ion	Calcium Ion	Oxide	Oxide
Calcium Ion	Calcium Ion	Oxide	Oxide

O^{-2}	O^{-2}	Ca^{+2}	Ca^{+2}
O^{-2}	O^{-2}	Ca^{+2}	Ca^{+2}

Ion Flashcards

| Phosphate | Phosphate | Phosphate | Phosphate |

$(PO_4)^{-3}$ $(PO_4)^{-3}$ $(PO_4)^{-3}$ $(PO_4)^{-3}$

Aluminum Ion	Aluminum Ion	Aluminum Ion	Aluminum Ion

Al^{+3} Al^{+3} Al^{+3} Al^{+3}

| Chromium Ion | Chromium Ion | Chromium Ion | Chromium Ion |

Cr^{+3} | Cr^{+3} | Cr^{+3} | Cr^{+3}

| Lead (IV) Ion | Lead (IV) Ion | Lead (IV) Ion | Lead (IV) Ion |

Pb^{+4} Pb^{+4} Pb^{+4} Pb^{+4}

Tin (IV) Ion	Tin (IV) Ion	Tin (IV) Ion	Tin (IV) Ion

Sn^{+4} Sn^{+4} Sn^{+4} Sn^{+4}

Ion Flashcards

Element Flash Cards	Element Flash Cards	Element Flash Cards
Hydrogen	**Beryllium**	**Nitrogen**
Element Flash Cards	Element Flash Cards	Element Flash Cards
Helium	**Boron**	**Oxygen**
Element Flash Cards	Element Flash Cards	Element Flash Cards
Lithium	**Carbon**	**Fluorine**

Element Flash Cards	Element Flash Cards	Element Flash Cards
N	Be	H
Element Flash Cards	Element Flash Cards	Element Flash Cards
O	B	He
Element Flash Cards	Element Flash Cards	Element Flash Cards
F	C	Li

Element Flash Card Set

Element Flash Cards	Element Flash Cards	Element Flash Cards
Neon	**Aluminum**	**Sulfur**
Element Flash Cards	Element Flash Cards	Element Flash Cards
Sodium	**Silicon**	**Chlorine**
Element Flash Cards	Element Flash Cards	Element Flash Cards
Magnesium	**Phosphorus**	**Argon**

Element Flash Cards	Element Flash Cards	Element Flash Cards
S	Al	Ne
Element Flash Cards	Element Flash Cards	Element Flash Cards
Cl	Si	Na
Element Flash Cards	Element Flash Cards	Element Flash Cards
Ar	P	Mg

Element Flash Card Set

Element Flash Cards	Element Flash Cards	Element Flash Cards
Potassium	**Titanium**	**Manganese**
Element Flash Cards	Element Flash Cards	Element Flash Cards
Calcium	**Vanadium**	**Iron**
Element Flash Cards	Element Flash Cards	Element Flash Cards
Scandium	**Chromium**	**Cobalt**

Element Flash Cards	**Element Flash Cards**	**Element Flash Cards**
Mn	Ti	K
Element Flash Cards	**Element Flash Cards**	**Element Flash Cards**
Fe	V	Ca
Element Flash Cards	**Element Flash Cards**	**Element Flash Cards**
Co	Cr	Sc

Element Flash Card Set

Element Flash Cards	Element Flash Cards	Element Flash Cards
Rubidium	**Zirconium**	**Technetium**
Element Flash Cards	Element Flash Cards	Element Flash Cards
Strontium	**Niobium**	**Ruthenium**
Element Flash Cards	Element Flash Cards	Element Flash Cards
Yttrium	**Molybdenum**	**Rhodium**

Element Flash Cards	Element Flash Cards	Element Flash Cards
Tc	Zr	Rb
Element Flash Cards	Element Flash Cards	Element Flash Cards
Ru	Nb	Sr
Element Flash Cards	Element Flash Cards	Element Flash Cards
Rh	Mo	Y

Element Flash Card Set

Element Flash Cards	Element Flash Cards	Element Flash Cards
Nickel	**Gallium**	**Selenium**
Element Flash Cards	Element Flash Cards	Element Flash Cards
Copper	**Germanium**	**Bromine**
Element Flash Cards	Element Flash Cards	Element Flash Cards
Zinc	**Arsenic**	**Krypton**

Element Flash Cards	**Element Flash Cards**	**Element Flash Cards**
Se	Ga	Ni
Element Flash Cards	**Element Flash Cards**	**Element Flash Cards**
Br	Ge	Cu
Element Flash Cards	**Element Flash Cards**	**Element Flash Cards**
Kr	As	Zn

Element Flash Card Set

Element Flash Cards	Element Flash Cards	Element Flash Cards
Palladium	**Indium**	**Tellurium**
Element Flash Cards	Element Flash Cards	Element Flash Cards
Silver	**Tin**	**Iodine**
Element Flash Cards	Element Flash Cards	Element Flash Cards
Cadmium	**Antimony**	**Xenon**

Element Flash Cards	Element Flash Cards	Element Flash Cards
Te	In	Pd
Element Flash Cards	Element Flash Cards	Element Flash Cards
I	Sn	Ag
Element Flash Cards	Element Flash Cards	Element Flash Cards
Xe	Sb	Cd

Element Flash Card Set

Compound Intensity!	*Compound Intensity!*	*Compound Intensity!*
CATION	**CATION**	**CATION**
Compound Intensity!	*Compound Intensity!*	*Compound Intensity!*
CATION	**CATION**	**CATION**
Compound Intensity!	*Compound Intensity!*	*Compound Intensity!*
CATION	**CATION**	**CATION**

Compound Intensity!	*Compound Intensity!*	*Compound Intensity!*
Barium Ion **6 points**	**Silver Ion** **10 points**	**Ammonium Ion** **15 points**
Compound Intensity!	*Compound Intensity!*	*Compound Intensity!*
NIckel Ion **10 points**	**Zinc Ion** **10 points**	**Aluminum Ion** **10 points**
Compound Intensity!	*Compound Intensity!*	*Compound Intensity!*
Chromium Ion **10 points**	**Lead (II) Ion** **14 points**	**Tin (IV) Ion** **14 points**

Compound Intensity!	*Compound Intensity!*	*Compound Intensity!*
CATION	**CATION**	**CATION**
Compound Intensity!	*Compound Intensity!*	*Compound Intensity!*
CATION	**CATION**	**CATION**
Compound Intensity!	*Compound Intensity!*	*Compound Intensity!*
CATION	**CATION**	**CATION**

Compound Intensity! **Tin (II) Ion** **14 points**	*Compound Intensity!* **Wild Cation!** **20 points**	*Compound Intensity!* _____ **____ points**
Compound Intensity! _____ **____ points**	*Compound Intensity!* _____ **____ points**	*Compound Intensity!* _____ **____ points**
Compound Intensity! _____ **____ points**	*Compound Intensity!* _____ **____ points**	*Compound Intensity!* _____ **____ points**

Compound Intensity!	*Compound Intensity!*	*Compound Intensity!*
CATION	*CATION*	*CATION*
Compound Intensity!	*Compound Intensity!*	*Compound Intensity!*
CATION	*CATION*	*CATION*
Compound Intensity!	*Compound Intensity!*	*Compound Intensity!*
CATION	*CATION*	*CATION*

Compound Intensity! **Hydrogen Ion** **5 points**	*Compound Intensity!* **Lithium Ion** **5 points**	*Compound Intensity!* **Sodium Ion** **6 points**
Compound Intensity! **Potassium Ion** **6 points**	*Compound Intensity!* **Calcium Ion** **6 points**	*Compound Intensity!* **Copper (II) Ion** **12 points**
Compound Intensity! **Magnesium Ion** **6 points**	*Compound Intensity!* **Iron (III) Ion** **12 points**	*Compound Intensity!* **Lead (IV) Ion** **15 points**

Compound Intensity Card Set

Compound Intensity!	*Compound Intensity!*	*Compound Intensity!*
ANION	**ANION**	**ANION**
Compound Intensity!	*Compound Intensity!*	*Compound Intensity!*
ANION	**ANION**	**ANION**
Compound Intensity!	*Compound Intensity!*	*Compound Intensity!*
ANION	**ANION**	**ANION**

Compound Intensity Card Set

Compound Intensity! **Fluoride** **5 points**	*Compound Intensity!* **Chloride Ion** **5 points**	*Compound Intensity!* **Peroxide Ion** **12 points**
Compound Intensity! **Carbonate** **15 points**	*Compound Intensity!* **Oxide** **5 points**	*Compound Intensity!* **Sulfide** **6 points**
Compound Intensity! **Hypochlorite** **12 points**	*Compound Intensity!* **Chlorite** **10 points**	*Compound Intensity!* **Chlorate** **10 points**

Compound Intensity Card Set

Compound Intensity!	*Compound Intensity!*	*Compound Intensity!*
ANION	***ANION***	***ANION***
Compound Intensity!	*Compound Intensity!*	*Compound Intensity!*
ANION	***ANION***	***ANION***
Compound Intensity!	*Compound Intensity!*	*Compound Intensity!*
ANION	***ANION***	***ANION***

Compound Intensity! **Cyanide** **8 points**	*Compound Intensity!* **Bromide Ion** **5 points**	*Compound Intensity!* _____ ____ *points*
Compound Intensity! _____ ____ *points*	*Compound Intensity!* _____ ____ *points*	*Compound Intensity!* _____ ____ *points*
Compound Intensity! _____ ____ *points*	*Compound Intensity!* _____ ____ *points*	*Compound Intensity!* _____ ____ *points*

Compound Intensity Card Set

Compound Intensity!	*Compound Intensity!*	*Compound Intensity!*
ANION	*ANION*	*ANION*
Compound Intensity!	*Compound Intensity!*	*Compound Intensity!*
ANION	*ANION*	*ANION*
Compound Intensity!	*Compound Intensity!*	*Compound Intensity!*
ANION	*ANION*	*ANION*

Compound Intensity!	*Compound Intensity!*	*Compound Intensity!*
Wild Anion! *18 points*	*Hydroxide* *5 points*	*Nitrite* *10 points*
Compound Intensity!	*Compound Intensity!*	*Compound Intensity!*
Nitrate *10 points*	*Sulfite* *10 points*	*Sulfate* *10 points*
Compound Intensity!	*Compound Intensity!*	*Compound Intensity!*
Phosphate *12 points*	*Permanganate* *15 points*	*Iodide* *5 points*

Compound Intensity Card Set

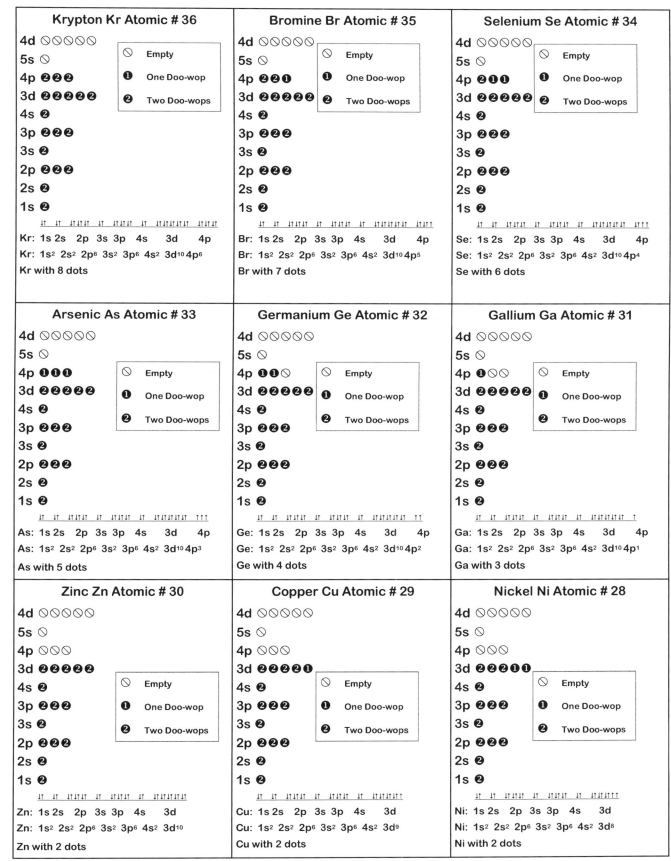

Krypton Kr Atomic # 36

4d ⊘⊘⊘⊘⊘
5s ⊘
4p ❷❷❷
3d ❷❷❷❷❷
4s ❷
3p ❷❷❷
3s ❷
2p ❷❷❷
2s ❷
1s ❷

⊘	Empty
❶	One Doo-wop
❷	Two Doo-wops

⇅ ⇅ ⇅⇅⇅ ⇅ ⇅⇅⇅ ⇅ ⇅⇅⇅⇅⇅ ⇅⇅⇅

Kr: 1s 2s 2p 3s 3p 4s   3d   4p

Kr: $1s^2$ $2s^2$ $2p^6$ $3s^2$ $3p^6$ $4s^2$ $3d^{10}$ $4p^6$

Kr with 8 dots

Bromine Br Atomic # 35

4d ⊘⊘⊘⊘⊘
5s ⊘
4p ❷❷❶
3d ❷❷❷❷❷
4s ❷
3p ❷❷❷
3s ❷
2p ❷❷❷
2s ❷
1s ❷

⊘	Empty
❶	One Doo-wop
❷	Two Doo-wops

⇅ ⇅ ⇅⇅⇅ ⇅ ⇅⇅⇅ ⇅ ⇅⇅⇅⇅⇅ ⇅⇅↑

Br: 1s 2s 2p 3s 3p 4s   3d   4p

Br: $1s^2$ $2s^2$ $2p^6$ $3s^2$ $3p^6$ $4s^2$ $3d^{10}$ $4p^5$

Br with 7 dots

Selenium Se Atomic # 34

4d ⊘⊘⊘⊘⊘
5s ⊘
4p ❷❶❶
3d ❷❷❷❷❷
4s ❷
3p ❷❷❷
3s ❷
2p ❷❷❷
2s ❷
1s ❷

⊘	Empty
❶	One Doo-wop
❷	Two Doo-wops

⇅ ⇅ ⇅⇅⇅ ⇅ ⇅⇅⇅ ⇅ ⇅⇅⇅⇅⇅ ⇅↑↑

Se: 1s 2s 2p 3s 3p 4s   3d   4p

Se: $1s^2$ $2s^2$ $2p^6$ $3s^2$ $3p^6$ $4s^2$ $3d^{10}$ $4p^4$

Se with 6 dots

Arsenic As Atomic # 33

4d ⊘⊘⊘⊘⊘
5s ⊘
4p ❶❶❶
3d ❷❷❷❷❷
4s ❷
3p ❷❷❷
3s ❷
2p ❷❷❷
2s ❷
1s ❷

⊘	Empty
❶	One Doo-wop
❷	Two Doo-wops

⇅ ⇅ ⇅⇅⇅ ⇅ ⇅⇅⇅ ⇅ ⇅⇅⇅⇅⇅ ↑↑↑

As: 1s 2s 2p 3s 3p 4s   3d   4p

As: $1s^2$ $2s^2$ $2p^6$ $3s^2$ $3p^6$ $4s^2$ $3d^{10}$ $4p^3$

As with 5 dots

Germanium Ge Atomic # 32

4d ⊘⊘⊘⊘⊘
5s ⊘
4p ❶❶⊘
3d ❷❷❷❷❷
4s ❷
3p ❷❷❷
3s ❷
2p ❷❷❷
2s ❷
1s ❷

⊘	Empty
❶	One Doo-wop
❷	Two Doo-wops

⇅ ⇅ ⇅⇅⇅ ⇅ ⇅⇅⇅ ⇅ ⇅⇅⇅⇅⇅ ↑↑

Ge: 1s 2s 2p 3s 3p 4s   3d   4p

Ge: $1s^2$ $2s^2$ $2p^6$ $3s^2$ $3p^6$ $4s^2$ $3d^{10}$ $4p^2$

Ge with 4 dots

Gallium Ga Atomic # 31

4d ⊘⊘⊘⊘⊘
5s ⊘
4p ❶⊘⊘
3d ❷❷❷❷❷
4s ❷
3p ❷❷❷
3s ❷
2p ❷❷❷
2s ❷
1s ❷

⊘	Empty
❶	One Doo-wop
❷	Two Doo-wops

⇅ ⇅ ⇅⇅⇅ ⇅ ⇅⇅⇅ ⇅ ⇅⇅⇅⇅⇅ ↑

Ga: 1s 2s 2p 3s 3p 4s   3d   4p

Ga: $1s^2$ $2s^2$ $2p^6$ $3s^2$ $3p^6$ $4s^2$ $3d^{10}$ $4p^1$

Ga with 3 dots

Zinc Zn Atomic # 30

4d ⊘⊘⊘⊘⊘
5s ⊘
4p ⊘⊘⊘
3d ❷❷❷❷❷
4s ❷
3p ❷❷❷
3s ❷
2p ❷❷❷
2s ❷
1s ❷

⊘	Empty
❶	One Doo-wop
❷	Two Doo-wops

⇅ ⇅ ⇅⇅⇅ ⇅ ⇅⇅⇅ ⇅ ⇅⇅⇅⇅⇅

Zn: 1s 2s 2p 3s 3p 4s   3d

Zn: $1s^2$ $2s^2$ $2p^6$ $3s^2$ $3p^6$ $4s^2$ $3d^{10}$

Zn with 2 dots

Copper Cu Atomic # 29

4d ⊘⊘⊘⊘⊘
5s ⊘
4p ⊘⊘⊘
3d ❷❷❷❷❶
4s ❷
3p ❷❷❷
3s ❷
2p ❷❷❷
2s ❷
1s ❷

⊘	Empty
❶	One Doo-wop
❷	Two Doo-wops

⇅ ⇅ ⇅⇅⇅ ⇅ ⇅⇅⇅ ⇅ ⇅⇅⇅⇅↑

Cu: 1s 2s 2p 3s 3p 4s   3d

Cu: $1s^2$ $2s^2$ $2p^6$ $3s^2$ $3p^6$ $4s^2$ $3d^9$

Cu with 2 dots

Nickel Ni Atomic # 28

4d ⊘⊘⊘⊘⊘
5s ⊘
4p ⊘⊘⊘
3d ❷❷❷❶❶
4s ❷
3p ❷❷❷
3s ❷
2p ❷❷❷
2s ❷
1s ❷

⊘	Empty
❶	One Doo-wop
❷	Two Doo-wops

⇅ ⇅ ⇅⇅⇅ ⇅ ⇅⇅⇅ ⇅ ⇅⇅⇅↑↑

Ni: 1s 2s 2p 3s 3p 4s   3d

Ni: $1s^2$ $2s^2$ $2p^6$ $3s^2$ $3p^6$ $4s^2$ $3d^8$

Ni with 2 dots

Doo-Wop Mania	*Doo-Wop Mania*	*Doo-Wop Mania*
Selenium	**Bromine**	**Krypton**
Doo-Wop Mania	*Doo-Wop Mania*	*Doo-Wop Mania*
Gallium	**Germanium**	**Arsenic**
Doo-Wop Mania	*Doo-Wop Mania*	*Doo-Wop Mania*
Nickel	**Copper**	**Zinc**

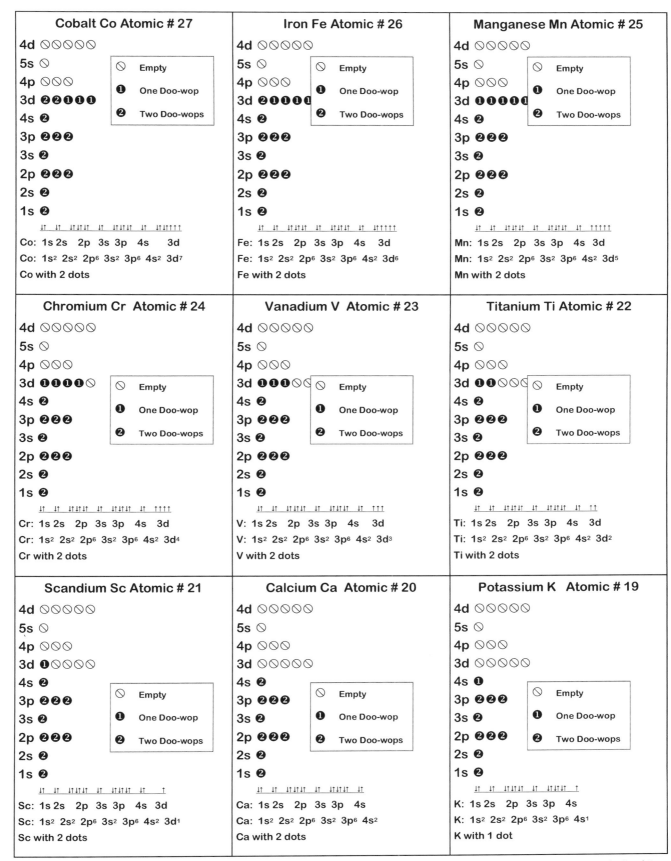

Cobalt Co Atomic # 27

4d ⊘⊘⊘⊘⊘
5s ⊘
4p ⊘⊘⊘
3d ❷❷❶❶❶
4s ❷
3p ❷❷❷
3s ❷
2p ❷❷❷
2s ❷
1s ❷

⇅ ⇅ ⇅⇅⇅ ⇅ ⇅⇅⇅ ⇅ ⇅⇅↑↑↑

⊘	Empty
❶	One Doo-wop
❷	Two Doo-wops

Co: 1s 2s 2p 3s 3p 4s 3d

Co: 1s² 2s² 2p⁶ 3s² 3p⁶ 4s² 3d⁷

Co with 2 dots

Iron Fe Atomic # 26

4d ⊘⊘⊘⊘⊘
5s ⊘
4p ⊘⊘⊘
3d ❷❶❶❶❶
4s ❷
3p ❷❷❷
3s ❷
2p ❷❷❷
2s ❷
1s ❷

⇅ ⇅ ⇅⇅⇅ ⇅ ⇅⇅⇅ ⇅ ↑↑↑↑↑

⊘	Empty
❶	One Doo-wop
❷	Two Doo-wops

Fe: 1s 2s 2p 3s 3p 4s 3d

Fe: 1s² 2s² 2p⁶ 3s² 3p⁶ 4s² 3d⁶

Fe with 2 dots

Manganese Mn Atomic # 25

4d ⊘⊘⊘⊘⊘
5s ⊘
4p ⊘⊘⊘
3d ❶❶❶❶❶
4s ❷
3p ❷❷❷
3s ❷
2p ❷❷❷
2s ❷
1s ❷

⇅ ⇅ ⇅⇅⇅ ⇅ ⇅⇅⇅ ⇅ ↑↑↑↑↑

⊘	Empty
❶	One Doo-wop
❷	Two Doo-wops

Mn: 1s 2s 2p 3s 3p 4s 3d

Mn: 1s² 2s² 2p⁶ 3s² 3p⁶ 4s² 3d⁵

Mn with 2 dots

Chromium Cr Atomic # 24

4d ⊘⊘⊘⊘⊘
5s ⊘
4p ⊘⊘⊘
3d ❶❶❶❶⊘
4s ❷
3p ❷❷❷
3s ❷
2p ❷❷❷
2s ❷
1s ❷

⇅ ⇅ ⇅⇅⇅ ⇅ ⇅⇅⇅ ⇅ ↑↑↑↑

⊘	Empty
❶	One Doo-wop
❷	Two Doo-wops

Cr: 1s 2s 2p 3s 3p 4s 3d

Cr: 1s² 2s² 2p⁶ 3s² 3p⁶ 4s² 3d⁴

Cr with 2 dots

Vanadium V Atomic # 23

4d ⊘⊘⊘⊘⊘
5s ⊘
4p ⊘⊘⊘
3d ❶❶❶⊘⊘
4s ❷
3p ❷❷❷
3s ❷
2p ❷❷❷
2s ❷
1s ❷

⇅ ⇅ ⇅⇅⇅ ⇅ ⇅⇅⇅ ⇅ ↑↑↑

⊘	Empty
❶	One Doo-wop
❷	Two Doo-wops

V: 1s 2s 2p 3s 3p 4s 3d

V: 1s² 2s² 2p⁶ 3s² 3p⁶ 4s² 3d³

V with 2 dots

Titanium Ti Atomic # 22

4d ⊘⊘⊘⊘⊘
5s ⊘
4p ⊘⊘⊘
3d ❶❶⊘⊘⊘
4s ❷
3p ❷❷❷
3s ❷
2p ❷❷❷
2s ❷
1s ❷

⇅ ⇅ ⇅⇅⇅ ⇅ ⇅⇅⇅ ⇅ ↑↑

⊘	Empty
❶	One Doo-wop
❷	Two Doo-wops

Ti: 1s 2s 2p 3s 3p 4s 3d

Ti: 1s² 2s² 2p⁶ 3s² 3p⁶ 4s² 3d²

Ti with 2 dots

Scandium Sc Atomic # 21

4d ⊘⊘⊘⊘⊘
5s ⊘
4p ⊘⊘⊘
3d ❶⊘⊘⊘⊘
4s ❷
3p ❷❷❷
3s ❷
2p ❷❷❷
2s ❷
1s ❷

⇅ ⇅ ⇅⇅⇅ ⇅ ⇅⇅⇅ ⇅ ↑

⊘	Empty
❶	One Doo-wop
❷	Two Doo-wops

Sc: 1s 2s 2p 3s 3p 4s 3d

Sc: 1s² 2s² 2p⁶ 3s² 3p⁶ 4s² 3d¹

Sc with 2 dots

Calcium Ca Atomic # 20

4d ⊘⊘⊘⊘⊘
5s ⊘
4p ⊘⊘⊘
3d ⊘⊘⊘⊘⊘
4s ❷
3p ❷❷❷
3s ❷
2p ❷❷❷
2s ❷
1s ❷

⇅ ⇅ ⇅⇅⇅ ⇅ ⇅⇅⇅ ⇅

⊘	Empty
❶	One Doo-wop
❷	Two Doo-wops

Ca: 1s 2s 2p 3s 3p 4s

Ca: 1s² 2s² 2p⁶ 3s² 3p⁶ 4s²

Ca with 2 dots

Potassium K Atomic # 19

4d ⊘⊘⊘⊘⊘
5s ⊘
4p ⊘⊘⊘
3d ⊘⊘⊘⊘⊘
4s ❶
3p ❷❷❷
3s ❷
2p ❷❷❷
2s ❷
1s ❷

⇅ ⇅ ⇅⇅⇅ ⇅ ⇅⇅⇅ ↑

⊘	Empty
❶	One Doo-wop
❷	Two Doo-wops

K: 1s 2s 2p 3s 3p 4s

K: 1s² 2s² 2p⁶ 3s² 3p⁶ 4s¹

K with 1 dot

Doo-Wop Mania	*Doo-Wop Mania*	*Doo-Wop Mania*
Manganese	**Iron**	**Cobalt**
Doo-Wop Mania	*Doo-Wop Mania*	*Doo-Wop Mania*
Titanium	**Vanadium**	**Chromium**
Doo-Wop Mania	*Doo-Wop Mania*	*Doo-Wop Mania*
Potassium	**Calcium**	**Scandium**

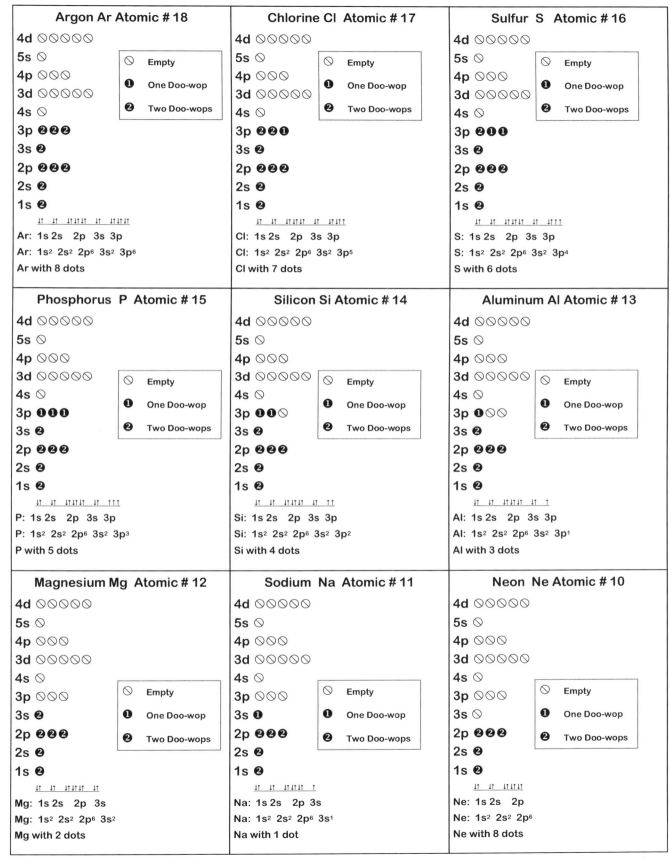

Argon Ar Atomic # 18

4d ◌◌◌◌◌
5s ◌
4p ◌◌◌
3d ◌◌◌◌◌
4s ◌
3p ❷❷❷
3s ❷
2p ❷❷❷
2s ❷
1s ❷

◌ Empty
❶ One Doo-wop
❷ Two Doo-wops

↿⇂ ↿⇂ ↿⇂↿⇂↿⇂ ↿⇂ ↿⇂↿⇂↿⇂

Ar: 1s 2s 2p 3s 3p
Ar: 1s² 2s² 2p⁶ 3s² 3p⁶
Ar with 8 dots

Chlorine Cl Atomic # 17

4d ◌◌◌◌◌
5s ◌
4p ◌◌◌
3d ◌◌◌◌◌
4s ◌
3p ❷❷❶
3s ❷
2p ❷❷❷
2s ❷
1s ❷

◌ Empty
❶ One Doo-wop
❷ Two Doo-wops

↿⇂ ↿⇂ ↿⇂↿⇂↿⇂ ↿⇂ ↿⇂↿⇂↿

Cl: 1s 2s 2p 3s 3p
Cl: 1s² 2s² 2p⁶ 3s² 3p⁵
Cl with 7 dots

Sulfur S Atomic # 16

4d ◌◌◌◌◌
5s ◌
4p ◌◌◌
3d ◌◌◌◌◌
4s ◌
3p ❷❶❶
3s ❷
2p ❷❷❷
2s ❷
1s ❷

◌ Empty
❶ One Doo-wop
❷ Two Doo-wops

↿⇂ ↿⇂ ↿⇂↿⇂↿⇂ ↿⇂ ↿↿↿↿

S: 1s 2s 2p 3s 3p
S: 1s² 2s² 2p⁶ 3s² 3p⁴
S with 6 dots

Phosphorus P Atomic # 15

4d ◌◌◌◌◌
5s ◌
4p ◌◌◌
3d ◌◌◌◌◌
4s ◌
3p ❶❶❶
3s ❷
2p ❷❷❷
2s ❷
1s ❷

◌ Empty
❶ One Doo-wop
❷ Two Doo-wops

↿⇂ ↿⇂ ↿⇂↿⇂↿⇂ ↿⇂ ↿↿↿

P: 1s 2s 2p 3s 3p
P: 1s² 2s² 2p⁶ 3s² 3p³
P with 5 dots

Silicon Si Atomic # 14

4d ◌◌◌◌◌
5s ◌
4p ◌◌◌
3d ◌◌◌◌◌
4s ◌
3p ❶❶◌
3s ❷
2p ❷❷❷
2s ❷
1s ❷

◌ Empty
❶ One Doo-wop
❷ Two Doo-wops

↿⇂ ↿⇂ ↿⇂↿⇂↿⇂ ↿⇂ ↿↿

Si: 1s 2s 2p 3s 3p
Si: 1s² 2s² 2p⁶ 3s² 3p²
Si with 4 dots

Aluminum Al Atomic # 13

4d ◌◌◌◌◌
5s ◌
4p ◌◌◌
3d ◌◌◌◌◌
4s ◌
3p ❶◌◌
3s ❷
2p ❷❷❷
2s ❷
1s ❷

◌ Empty
❶ One Doo-wop
❷ Two Doo-wops

↿⇂ ↿⇂ ↿⇂↿⇂↿⇂ ↿⇂ ↿

Al: 1s 2s 2p 3s 3p
Al: 1s² 2s² 2p⁶ 3s² 3p¹
Al with 3 dots

Magnesium Mg Atomic # 12

4d ◌◌◌◌◌
5s ◌
4p ◌◌◌
3d ◌◌◌◌◌
4s ◌
3p ◌◌◌
3s ❷
2p ❷❷❷
2s ❷
1s ❷

◌ Empty
❶ One Doo-wop
❷ Two Doo-wops

↿⇂ ↿⇂ ↿⇂↿⇂↿⇂ ↿⇂

Mg: 1s 2s 2p 3s
Mg: 1s² 2s² 2p⁶ 3s²
Mg with 2 dots

Sodium Na Atomic # 11

4d ◌◌◌◌◌
5s ◌
4p ◌◌◌
3d ◌◌◌◌◌
4s ◌
3p ◌◌◌
3s ❶
2p ❷❷❷
2s ❷
1s ❷

◌ Empty
❶ One Doo-wop
❷ Two Doo-wops

↿⇂ ↿⇂ ↿⇂↿⇂↿⇂ ↿

Na: 1s 2s 2p 3s
Na: 1s² 2s² 2p⁶ 3s¹
Na with 1 dot

Neon Ne Atomic # 10

4d ◌◌◌◌◌
5s ◌
4p ◌◌◌
3d ◌◌◌◌◌
4s ◌
3p ◌◌◌
3s ◌
2p ❷❷❷
2s ❷
1s ❷

◌ Empty
❶ One Doo-wop
❷ Two Doo-wops

↿⇂ ↿⇂ ↿⇂↿⇂↿⇂

Ne: 1s 2s 2p
Ne: 1s² 2s² 2p⁶
Ne with 8 dots

Doo-Wop Mania Card Set

Doo-Wop Mania

Sulfur

Doo-Wop Mania

Chlorine

Doo-Wop Mania

Argon

Doo-Wop Mania

Aluminum

Doo-Wop Mania

Silicon

Doo-Wop Mania

Phosphorus

Doo-Wop Mania

Neon

Doo-Wop Mania

Sodium

Doo-Wop Mania

Magnesium

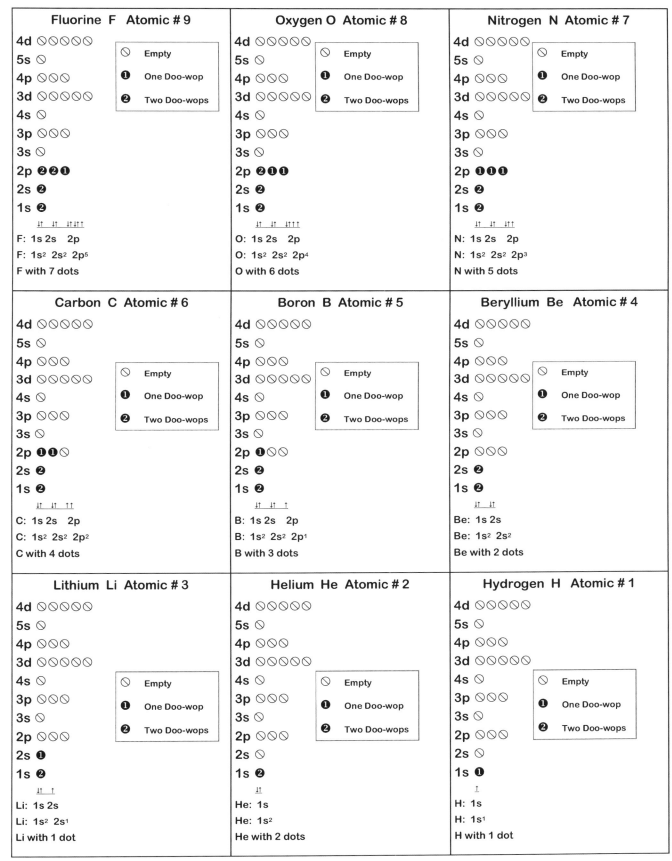

Fluorine F Atomic # 9

4d ⊘⊘⊘⊘⊘
5s ⊘
4p ⊘⊘⊘
3d ⊘⊘⊘⊘⊘
4s ⊘
3p ⊘⊘⊘
3s ⊘
2p ❷❷❶
2s ❷
1s ❷

⊘	Empty
❶	One Doo-wop
❷	Two Doo-wops

↓↑ ↓↑ ↓↑↓↑↑

F: 1s 2s 2p
F: 1s² 2s² 2p⁵
F with 7 dots

Oxygen O Atomic # 8

4d ⊘⊘⊘⊘⊘
5s ⊘
4p ⊘⊘⊘
3d ⊘⊘⊘⊘⊘
4s ⊘
3p ⊘⊘⊘
3s ⊘
2p ❷❶❶
2s ❷
1s ❷

⊘	Empty
❶	One Doo-wop
❷	Two Doo-wops

↓↑ ↓↑ ↓↑↓↑↑

O: 1s 2s 2p
O: 1s² 2s² 2p⁴
O with 6 dots

Nitrogen N Atomic # 7

4d ⊘⊘⊘⊘⊘
5s ⊘
4p ⊘⊘⊘
3d ⊘⊘⊘⊘⊘
4s ⊘
3p ⊘⊘⊘
3s ⊘
2p ❶❶❶
2s ❷
1s ❷

⊘	Empty
❶	One Doo-wop
❷	Two Doo-wops

↓↑ ↓↑ ↓↑↑

N: 1s 2s 2p
N: 1s² 2s² 2p³
N with 5 dots

Carbon C Atomic # 6

4d ⊘⊘⊘⊘⊘
5s ⊘
4p ⊘⊘⊘
3d ⊘⊘⊘⊘⊘
4s ⊘
3p ⊘⊘⊘
3s ⊘
2p ❶❶⊘
2s ❷
1s ❷

⊘	Empty
❶	One Doo-wop
❷	Two Doo-wops

↓↑ ↓↑ ↑↑

C: 1s 2s 2p
C: 1s² 2s² 2p²
C with 4 dots

Boron B Atomic # 5

4d ⊘⊘⊘⊘⊘
5s ⊘
4p ⊘⊘⊘
3d ⊘⊘⊘⊘⊘
4s ⊘
3p ⊘⊘⊘
3s ⊘
2p ❶⊘⊘
2s ❷
1s ❷

⊘	Empty
❶	One Doo-wop
❷	Two Doo-wops

↓↑ ↓↑ ↑

B: 1s 2s 2p
B: 1s² 2s² 2p¹
B with 3 dots

Beryllium Be Atomic # 4

4d ⊘⊘⊘⊘⊘
5s ⊘
4p ⊘⊘⊘
3d ⊘⊘⊘⊘⊘
4s ⊘
3p ⊘⊘⊘
3s ⊘
2p ⊘⊘⊘
2s ❷
1s ❷

⊘	Empty
❶	One Doo-wop
❷	Two Doo-wops

↓↑ ↓↑

Be: 1s 2s
Be: 1s² 2s²
Be with 2 dots

Lithium Li Atomic # 3

4d ⊘⊘⊘⊘⊘
5s ⊘
4p ⊘⊘⊘
3d ⊘⊘⊘⊘⊘
4s ⊘
3p ⊘⊘⊘
3s ⊘
2p ⊘⊘⊘
2s ❶
1s ❷

⊘	Empty
❶	One Doo-wop
❷	Two Doo-wops

↓↑ ↑

Li: 1s 2s
Li: 1s² 2s¹
Li with 1 dot

Helium He Atomic # 2

4d ⊘⊘⊘⊘⊘
5s ⊘
4p ⊘⊘⊘
3d ⊘⊘⊘⊘⊘
4s ⊘
3p ⊘⊘⊘
3s ⊘
2p ⊘⊘⊘
2s ⊘
1s ❷

⊘	Empty
❶	One Doo-wop
❷	Two Doo-wops

↓↑

He: 1s
He: 1s²
He with 2 dots

Hydrogen H Atomic # 1

4d ⊘⊘⊘⊘⊘
5s ⊘
4p ⊘⊘⊘
3d ⊘⊘⊘⊘⊘
4s ⊘
3p ⊘⊘⊘
3s ⊘
2p ⊘⊘⊘
2s ⊘
1s ❶

⊘	Empty
❶	One Doo-wop
❷	Two Doo-wops

↑

H: 1s
H: 1s¹
H with 1 dot

Doo-Wop Mania *Doo-Wop Mania* *Doo-Wop Mania*

Nitrogen **Oxygen** **Fluorine**

Doo-Wop Mania *Doo-Wop Mania* *Doo-Wop Mania*

Beryllium **Boron** **Carbon**

Doo-Wop Mania *Doo-Wop Mania* *Doo-Wop Mania*

Hydrogen **Helium** **Lithium**